Egypt

Camilla de la Bédoyère

WAYLAND

First published in 2012 by Wayland
Copyright Wayland 2012

Wayland
Hachette Children's Books
338 Euston Road
London NW1 3BH

Wayland Australia
Level 17/207 Kent Street,
Sydney, NSW 2000

Concept design: Jason Billin
Editor: Sonya Newland
Design: 320 Design Ltd
Picture research: Sonya Newland
Consultant: Elaine Jackson
Proofreading and index: Alice Harman

Produced for Wayland by
White-Thomson Publishing Ltd

www.wtpub.co.uk
+44 (0)843 2087 460

British Library Cataloguing in Publication Data

De la Bédoyère, Camilla.
Egypt. -- (Discover countries)
1. Egypt -- Juvenile literature.
I. Title II. Series
962'.056-dc23

ISBN-13: 978 0 7502 6933 9
Printed in China

Wayland is a division of Hachette Children's Books
an Hachette UK company
www.hachette.co.uk

All data in this book was researched in 2011
and has been collected from the latest sources available at that time.

Contents

Discovering Egypt

Egypt is the world's largest Arab nation and it occupies a key position in Africa, connecting the continent to the Middle East and Asia. Although a modern, vibrant and developing country, Egypt is most famous for its fascinating history. Mighty pharaohs once ruled the region, and their legacy attracts tourists from all over the world. Egypt is about four times larger than the United Kingdom, but most of the land is barren desert.

DID YOU KNOW?
The Egyptian national flag bears the image of Saladin's eagle. Saladin was a sultan of Egypt and a great Muslim hero. Saladin's eagle represents power, beauty and independence.

An ancient nation

Egypt may be mostly desert, but the River Nile runs through the country from south to north. People began building settlements along the banks of the Nile thousands of years ago, because the surrounding land is very fertile. Alexander the Great conquered the region in 323 BCE, and it was later ruled by the Romans.

After the Roman Empire collapsed, Egypt became part of the Byzantine Empire until the Arab Muslim armies invaded in 639 CE. The culture and language of Egypt were soon transformed. The country has continued to change and develop over many centuries. Even today, there are big changes taking place in Egypt.

This map shows Egypt's main cities, features and bordering countries.

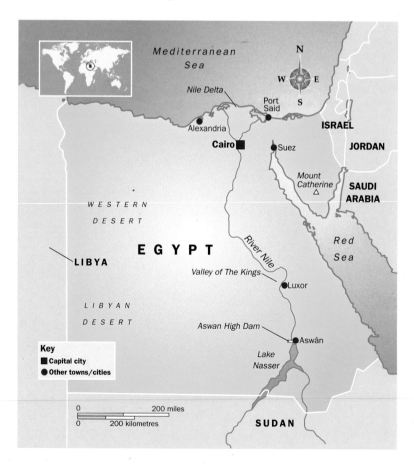

Changing times

By 2011, President Hosni Mubarak had ruled the nation for 30 years, and Egyptians began to protest against his system of government. When he came to power, Mubarak prevented people from expressing their political opinions. He controlled the newspapers and television, and maintained his power with the help of the police and the military. The Egyptian people rebelled, as part of a widespread political movement that became known as the 'Arab Spring'. A temporary government took control in Egypt, and democratic elections were organised.

Egypt Statistics

Area: 1,001,450 sq km (386,662 sq miles)
Capital city: Cairo
Government type: Republic
Bordering countries: Gaza Strip, Israel, Libya, Sudan
Currency: Egyptian pound
Language: Arabic (official), English and French widely understood

▼ As part of the Arab Spring in 2011, thousands of Egyptians gathered to protest about the way their country was run.

Landscape and climate

Egypt is a land of contrasts. While most of the landscape is desert and mountains, Egypt borders the Mediterranean Sea in the north and the Red Sea in the east. The whole of Egypt relies on the River Nile for water, food and transportation.

Egypt's lifeblood

The Nile is the longest river in the world. Its waters begin an incredible journey in East Africa and travel 6,650 km (4,132 miles). As the river reaches Egypt, its flow slows and it floods regularly. When rivers flood they deposit rich nutrients to the land, helping plants to flourish and grow. The Nile's mouth opens as a fertile delta, where the river splits up into many channels that often flood.

Facts at a glance

Land area: 995,450 sq km (384,345 sq miles)

Water area: 6,000 sq km (2,317 sq miles)

Highest point: Mount Catherine 2,629 m (8,625 ft)

Lowest point: Qattara Depression -133 m (-436 ft)

Longest river: Nile 1,200 km (750 miles) through Egypt; total: 6,650 km (4,132 miles)

Coastline: 2,450 km (1,522 miles)

▼ Egypt's most fertile farmland stretches along the banks of the Nile.

Deserts and sandstorms

Egypt's climate is hot and dry. This has caused the spread of huge desert areas, where rainfall is rare and few plants can survive. Without the Nile's fresh waters, the entire country would be desert, like its neighbour Libya. Egypt's extreme climate can lead to droughts and flash flooding.

Hot winds, known as the *Khamsin*, blow in from the Sahara Desert in the spring, bringing huge clouds of red dust to Egypt. Areas close to the Mediterranean Sea benefit from slightly higher rainfall and more pleasant temperatures than parts of the country further south.

Highlands

The Eastern Highlands and the Sinai mountains are areas of great natural beauty. This region of Egypt also marks a boundary between tectonic plates, so it is prone to earthquakes.

DID YOU KNOW?
The mountains in Sinai are mentioned in the Bible. It is here that Moses is said to have received two stone tablets from God, which were inscribed with the Ten Commandments.

◄ St Catherine's monastery lies at the foot of the 2,285-m (7,487-ft) Mount Sinai, in the Sinai Peninsula. It is one of the oldest working monasteries in the world.

▼ Typically, there is no rainfall in Cairo between June and October,

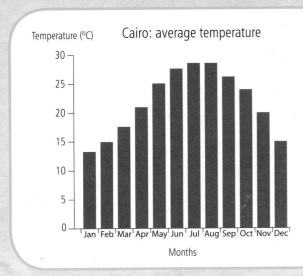

Cairo: average temperature

Temperature (ºC) / Months

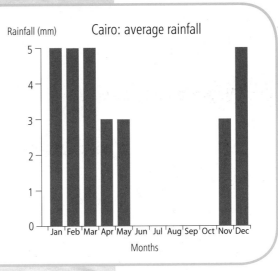

Cairo: average rainfall

Rainfall (mm) / Months

Most Egyptians can trace their ancestors back many generations within the country, especially in rural areas. There is little migration in or out of Egypt. The number of people in Egypt has risen rapidly in recent years, and it now has the fifteenth-largest population in the world.

Ethnic groups

The ethnic history of the Egyptian people contains both Arab and African influences. In the far south of the Nile Valley the people are mostly Nubians, who have a different culture to the Egyptians further north, with stronger links to an African heritage.

Bedouins are nomadic Arab people who live in Egypt and neighbouring regions. They often follow a traditional lifestyle, using ancient routes through the deserts to find grazing land and water for their animals. Although their traditional homes are tents made from animal skins, many modern Bedouins make their homes from stone or brick. Some Bedouin families have settled in towns.

> **Facts at a glance**
>
> **Total population:** 82.1 million
> **Life expectancy at birth:** 72.7 years
> **Children dying before the age of five:** 2.2%
> **Ethnic composition:** Egyptian 99.6%, other 0.4%

▶ This Nubian musician is playing a type of lyre, an ancient stringed instrument. What was once the ancient kingdom of Nubia now covers southern Egypt and northern Sudan.

A growing problem

Egypt's population stands at over 80 million, and has more than doubled since the 1970s. One-third of Egyptians are under 14 years old, which means that the rapid population growth is likely to continue as these young people have children of their own. Egypt's population may reach 123 million by 2050. This will put a strain on the country's resources, as it is difficult to provide food, water and services such as schools and health care for so many people.

Health matters

Sanitation and water supplies have improved greatly in recent years, and most people in the cities have access to clean water and toilets. However, the Nile and most other waterways are filthy. Dirty water contributes to the spread of infectious diseases, including diarrhoea, hepatitis A and typhoid. The health problems that most commonly cause death are heart disease, strokes, and liver and kidney diseases.

▼ Water pollution spreads disease in Egypt, as many people use waterways such as the Nile for washing and drinking water.

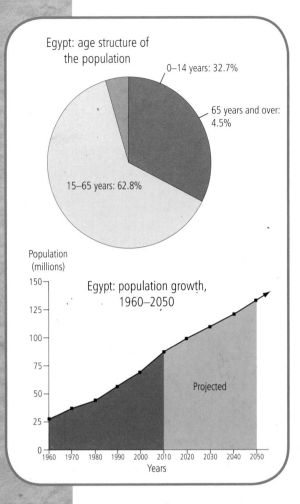

Egypt: age structure of the population

0–14 years: 32.7%

65 years and over: 4.5%

15–65 years: 62.8%

Population (millions)

Egypt: population growth, 1960–2050

Projected

Years

DID YOU KNOW?
Smoking causes nearly 200,000 deaths every year in Egypt, most of them men. People smoke cigarettes as well as the *sheesha*, or water pipe, which uses pipe tobacco.

Settlements and living

Egyptians live in a tiny part of the country's total land area – just four per cent of it. This is the land that surrounds the River Nile. As in many developing nations, the trend is for people to move away from the countryside and into towns. This means that urban areas in Egypt have grown to accommodate more people.

Sprawling cities

Most settlements have arisen along the Nile, where transport systems and fertile land are concentrated. In the 1950s, people in rural areas began to move to the towns and cities in search of work and a better quality of life. That trend is set to continue, and by 2020 it is likely that half of all Egyptians will live in towns.

Egypt's capital city, Cairo, is very densely populated, with at least 11 million people making their home in this sprawling but crowded city. The country's second city, Alexandria, has a population of about 4.4 million. Alexandria was Egypt's capital before the Islamic invasion in 639 CE.

Facts at a glance

Urban population: 42.8% (35.1 million)

Rural population: 57.2% (47 million)

Population of largest city: 11 million (Cairo)

▼ Cairo is the largest city in Africa, but despite its sprawling size it is still very overcrowded, with more than 30,000 people per square kilometre.

Big building projects

As people moved to the cities, houses were built quickly on any available piece of land. This led to extreme overcrowding, and slums grew up on the edges of the cities. There have been housing shortages in Cairo and Alexandria since the Second World War. Large-scale building projects have helped to improve urban life, but the speed of building has not kept pace with demand.

Rural homes

People who live in rural areas tend to have fewer luxuries than those who live in urban areas. They also have more limited access to the facilities of modern life, such as electricity and local hospitals.

Accommodation in rural areas is often simple. People rent land and then build their own homes from the materials that are around them, such as mud to make mud-bricks. The government, however, has worked to improve rural housing, and to supply utilities such as clean water and drainage.

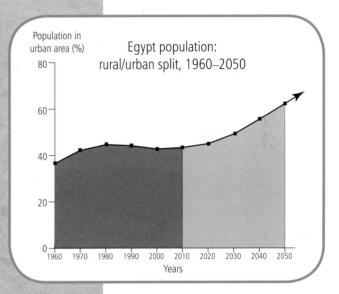

Egypt population: rural/urban split, 1960–2050

Population in urban area (%)

⬇ In rural settlements, houses and other buildings are constructed from wood or mud.

Family life

Family life is important to all Egyptians, regardless of where they live. Most Egyptians are Arabs, and follow Arab traditions in respect to family. In the nomadic groups, and in some rural areas, people remain very loyal to their tribes.

Women and marriage

Marrying young is not unusual in Arab countries, and one in ten Egyptian women marry before they are 20 years old. Most Egyptian women are married by the time they reach their mid-twenties.

Married women who live in towns are more likely to work outside the home than those who live on farms. In some rural areas, once a girl reaches the age of 16 she is expected to spend most of her time on household chores and looking after children.

▶ On the day before her wedding, an Egyptian bride is given henna tattoos on her hands and feet by her attendants.

A child's life

In both town and countryside, when a child is born the family will celebrate by slaughtering an animal (two for a boy, one for a girl) one week after the birth. The birth of a first son is a particularly joyful event. Boys are circumcised soon after they are born.

Extended families live together when there is enough room. In crowded Cairo apartments, nuclear families are more common. Children go to extra lessons after school to learn their faith, and spend time with relatives and friends. They must work hard at school so they can later study at the best colleges.

Changing society

Large families were once very common, but that is changing because many families find it hard to survive financially unless the mother is working too – especially in towns and cities. Since 2000, Egyptian women have been able to get divorced without their husband's agreement, but they give up all rights to the family's money. The care and custody of children also goes to the father when a couple divorces.

DID YOU KNOW? After the birth of a first son, the parents will often be called by the titles *Abu* ('father of') and *Umm* ('mother of') followed by the name of their son.

▼ In rural areas, large families are more common than in the cities, and older family members often live with their children and grandchildren.

Religion and beliefs

Long ago, Egyptians followed a religion that had many gods, and they regarded the sun as the source of all life. Today, 90 per cent of Egyptians follow the Islamic faith and way of life.

Islam in Egypt

Islamic armies brought the Muslim faith to Egypt nearly 1,400 years ago. The religion is part of everyday life for modern Egyptians. For example, its followers are called to prayer five times a day, and give money to those less well off than themselves. Many Muslim men still wear the traditional garment – a *galabiyah* – and women are expected to dress modestly. Some women wear long clothes and a veil when they leave the house.

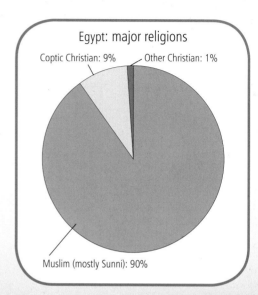

Egypt: major religions

Coptic Christian: 9%   Other Christian: 1%

Muslim (mostly Sunni): 90%

▼ Egyptian Muslims perform prayers five times a day, facing the direction of the holy city of Makkah in present-day Saudi Arabia.

Muslim festivals

Eid al-Adha is a four-day festival that celebrates the *Hajj,* or pilgrimage, to Makkah. During Ramadan, which falls in the ninth month of the Islamic year, Muslims fast from sunrise to sunset. Ramadan ends with a joyful celebration called Eid ul-Fitr. Other holy festivals, known as *moulids,* are often celebrated with street processions.

On the first day of Eid ul-Fitr, Muslims traditionally visit the graves of their relatives. Later, there are celebrations in the streets, where people sell sweets and toys.

Coptic Christians

Most Christians in Egypt follow the Coptic faith, which is similar to the Catholic faith. There are about nine million Copts in Egypt. Although they have the right to practise their religion without persecution, they have been the targets of discrimination and terrorist attacks in recent years.

Easter and Christmas are the most important festivals for Copts, as for other Christians. Followers of the faith also mark saints' days throughout the year, when the lives of holy people are remembered and celebrated.

DID YOU KNOW?
Nile Festival Day, or Wafaa an-Nil, has been celebrated since the time of the pharaohs. During this festival, there are parades and sporting events on the Nile.

Education and learning

As the number of children in Egypt keeps increasing, greater demands are being placed on the education system. The country has found it difficult to keep up with the growing need for schools, colleges and skilled teachers.

Better education

Before the mid-twentieth century, it was not unusual for Egyptians – especially women – to be illiterate. Since the 1950s, however, all children have been expected to go to primary school from the age of six. This education is free, and students have to stay at school until they are at least 12 years old.

Girls are only slightly less likely to go on to secondary school than boys, and an equal number of boys and girls go on to university. Wealthy families usually send their children to private schools and colleges.

Facts at a glance

Children in primary school:
Male 95%, Female 92%

Children in secondary school:
Male 66%, Female 64%

Literacy rate (over 15 years):
71.4 %

▼ Children in a primary-school class. Once they have finished the primary stage, they will receive their Basic Education Completion Certificate.

Moving on

At their primary school, children learn the key skills of reading, writing and maths. Those who pass the exams are able to move on to secondary school, where they study a wider range of subjects. There are two types of high school: general and technical.

At technical schools, students focus on vocational skills and learn about business, farming or industry. At general schools, students follow courses based on science, the arts (such as history and literature) and maths. Many students learn English and French as well as studying their native Arabic.

Learning for life

President Mubarak's government built new schools and universities, and set up projects to help adults learn to read and write. These efforts helped improve literacy in Egypt, but it has been difficult to keep pace with the increasing population, and Egypt's literacy rate is still among the lowest in the world.

◢ Students at the American University in Cairo. About 30 per cent of school leavers go on to higher education.

DID YOU KNOW? Two thousand years ago, the library at Alexandria was one of the world's earliest centres of learning. It was destroyed by the Romans, who burned it to the ground.

Employment and economy

The Egyptian government once guaranteed jobs for everyone. Today, however, nearly one in ten people is unemployed, and the workforce needs more technical skills to help the economy grow.

Types of work

Most working Egyptians are employed in the service industry, which includes tourism, transport, restaurants, banks and other financial firms. Many people work for the government because, in the past, all university graduates were promised jobs as civil servants. The government is still one of Egypt's largest employers. About one-third of all Egyptians are involved in agriculture.

Generally, salaries in Egypt are low. About 20 per cent of Egyptians live below the poverty line, which means they do not have enough money to buy all the basic necessities, such as food and clothes.

Facts at a glance

Contributions to GDP:
 agriculture: 13.5%
 industry: 37.9%
 services: 48.6%
Labour force:
 agriculture: 32%
 industry: 17%
 services: 51%
Female labour force:
 23% of total
Unemployment rate: 9%

▼ Tourism is an important part of the Egyptian economy. Official tourist workers and informal workers like this spice seller all benefit from Egypt's many foreign visitors.

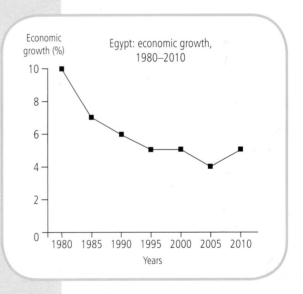

Informal trade is common in Egypt's cities. This old man is selling copies of the Qur'an – the holy book of Islam – on his street stall.

Informal work

Much work in Egypt is done on an informal basis. This means that the money earned from this work is not declared to the government, so no tax is paid on it. 'Informal work' includes unregistered businesses, self-employed manufacturers, taxi drivers and street vendors. One of the reasons for the huge informal economy is that it is complicated and expensive to set up a formal (legal) business in Egypt. It can take years to follow all the regulations that are needed to start a new business.

Working women

More women work in Egypt now than ever before. In 2003, 15 per cent of the workforce was female, but that has risen to 23 per cent in recent years. Women are most likely to work in service industries and agriculture.

Many women work at home, looking after the house and family. Unemployment is a particular problem for young women aged 18–29, and fewer than 20 per cent of them are in paid work.

DID YOU KNOW?

Egypt has a thriving film industry, and once was called the Hollywood of the Arab world. About three-quarters of all Arabic films are made in Egypt.

Industry and trade

The wealthiest countries are ones that export (sell) more goods than they import (buy). Egypt is a developing country and, although it has a wide range of industries, it still imports more goods than it exports.

Making wealth

In manufacturing industries, raw products such as cotton or steel are turned into goods, such as clothes or cars. Making goods in this way, and selling them, helps to create jobs and wealth – for people and for the country.

Until recently, the government owned most of the large manufacturing businesses in Egypt. In order to make businesses more efficient and profitable, most of them have now been sold to private companies.

DID YOU KNOW?
Cotton and the products made from it account for nearly a quarter of all Egypt's exports. These products include clothes, bed linen and towels.

Workers sew clothes in a cotton factory. Egyptian cotton is famous all over the world.

▶ The hydroelectric power station on the Aswan High Dam once produced more than half of Egypt's electricity. Output has been unable to keep pace with demand, though.

Energy to grow

Egypt benefits from cheap, renewable hydroelectricity, which is generated by water that flows through the huge turbines of the Aswan High Dam. Demand for energy, however, is growing so quickly that the dam can only supply a small amount of the electricity required.

There are large natural resources of fossil fuels in Egypt. Oil and natural gas help fuel Egypt's industries, and they are also sold to neighbouring countries. Eighty per cent of Egypt's electricity is generated by burning natural gas in power plants.

World trade

Egypt is one of the world's most important manufacturers of cotton fabric, from cotton plants. The sale of steel and building products, cars, paper, and products made from petrochemicals (such as oil) also help to drive the economy forwards.

Egypt exports many of its manufactured products, especially to the USA and Italy. The country's main exports are petroleum, and products made from petroleum. Egypt's main imports are raw materials to be turned into other products, pharmaceuticals (medicines), wheat, maize and steel.

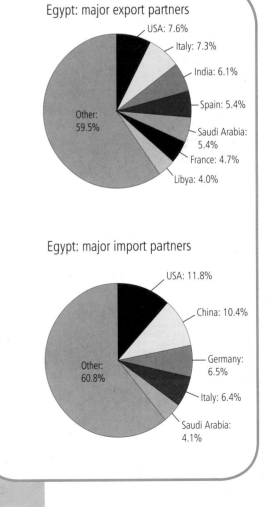

Egypt: major export partners

- USA: 7.6%
- Italy: 7.3%
- India: 6.1%
- Spain: 5.4%
- Saudi Arabia: 5.4%
- France: 4.7%
- Libya: 4.0%
- Other: 59.5%

Egypt: major import partners

- USA: 11.8%
- China: 10.4%
- Germany: 6.5%
- Italy: 6.4%
- Saudi Arabia: 4.1%
- Other: 60.8%

Farming and food

Only a tiny fraction of Egypt's land is available for farming – along the banks of the Nile. However, this region is extremely fertile, providing work and food for millions of Egyptian people.

The fertile Nile

The Nile had a long history of flooding, when the land would be inundated with water and natural fertilizers. The flooding was inconsistent, though, and droughts were common. In 1970, the Aswan High Dam was completed and it began to control the Nile's annual floods.

This dam holds back the Nile's floodwaters, releasing water only when it is needed. However, farmers now rely on expensive artificial fertilizers, because the Nile's nutrients can no longer reach the land.

▶ This woman is harvesting potatoes close to the Nile. More than 50 per cent of working women in Egypt have jobs in agriculture.

Top crops

The most important crops in Egypt are field crops, such as cotton and maize. They make up about three-quarters of all the farming produce. Livestock, such as cows, sheep and goats, fruit and vegetable crops account for the remainder. Thanks to the hot climate and irrigation schemes, most farmers are able to get two harvests from their land every year.

Fishing for food

Fish are taken from the Red Sea, the Mediterranean Sea, the Nile and other freshwater areas. Lake Nasser – a huge artificial lake created by the dam – has proved to be an excellent habitat for many fish, including the Nile perch.

Egyptian food

Egyptian food staples include bread and rice, but vegetables, beans and pulses are also important in an Egyptian's diet.

⬇ Fishermen on the Nile. The building of the Aswan High Dam altered the nature of the Nile, and it no longer holds as many fish as it used to.

Facts at a glance

Farmland: 4% of total land area

Main agricultural exports: Oranges, potatoes, molasses, rice, onions, cotton

Main agricultural imports: Wheat, maize, soy beans, raw sugar, palm oil

Average daily calorie intake: 3,325 calories

DID YOU KNOW? Falafels are deep-fried nuggets made from chickpeas and spices, served in pitta bread. They originated in Egypt, but they are now sold all over the world.

Transport and communications

The transport systems that operate in Egypt are a mixture of ancient and modern: donkeys pull carts, while jet planes zoom across the sky overhead.

Road, rail and air

Road-building can be an expensive process and while Egypt's major roads are modern, smaller roads that run through deserts and rural areas are often unpaved. Taxis, cars, buses, lorries and bicycles are used throughout the country, but a donkey or horse pulling a cart laden with farm produce is also a common sight in rural areas.

There are good rail links between the major ports and cities, and a metro system operates in Cairo. The international airport in Cairo is being developed to enable it to cope with an even greater number of flights, because it is an important hub for air traffic in the Middle East.

▼ In Cairo, road congestion is a huge problem and giant traffic jams clog up parts of the city for hours at a time. This contributes to the city's pollution problems.

Water transport

Egypt's first canal was built around 4,380 years ago, and now an extensive network of canals connects to the Nile, providing 3,200 km (1,988 miles) of navigable water routes. The Suez Canal is one of the world's most important waterways, and links the Red Sea to the Mediterranean. Ships use the canal to travel between European waters and the Indian and western Pacific Oceans.

▼ The Nile has been used to transport people and goods for thousands of years. Traditional Nile boats rely on wind power, and are called feluccas.

Facts at a glance

Total roads: 65,050 km (40,420 miles)
Paved roads: 47,500 km (29,515 miles)
Railways: 5,083 km (3,158 miles)
Major airports: 4
Major ports: Ayn Sukhnah, Alexandria, Damietta, El Dekheila, Port Said, Sidi Kurayr, Suez

Modern telecoms

In 1998, Egypt launched its communications satellite, Nilesat. It was the first Arab country to have one. Access to international television stations, mobile phones and the internet played a part in the Arab Spring and the downfall of President Mubarak's government in 2011.

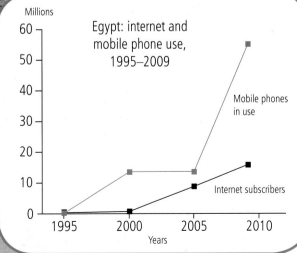

Egypt: internet and mobile phone use, 1995–2009

Leisure and tourism

In the strong Egyptian heat, a slow, leisurely pace is best, and Egyptians usually spend their free time relaxing. They meet up with friends, and shop in the evenings, when it is slightly cooler.

Friends and family

In Arabic societies men and women often socialize separately, and this custom is common in Egypt. Men meet in cafés to play games, drink tea and smoke, gathered around the *sheesha*, or water pipe. Women gather in homes to chat and enjoy shopping trips in city malls or the busy, colourful bazaars. During the holy time of Ramadan, watching television becomes an essential part of most families' leisure time.

▶ Children spend their leisure time with friends, and a game of football is a popular pastime.

Facts at a glance

Tourist arrivals (millions)

Year	Arrivals
1995	2.9
2000	5.5
2005	8.2
2009	11.9

Sports

Soccer, or football, is the national sport. The Egyptian national team is based in Cairo, and won the Africa Cup of Nations in 2010. For many Egyptian women, taking part in sports is difficult. Here, as in many other Muslim countries, sport is often regarded as an inappropriate leisure activity for females.

Ancient civilization

The discovery of King Tutankhamun's tomb in 1922 inspired the modern era of tourism in Egypt. His burial site had not been disturbed by tomb-raiders, and its intact treasures included beautiful masks of gold, and everyday objects that provided great historical information.

Millions of international travellers visit Egypt every year to discover more about the country's fascinating ancient history and to admire the temples, burial chambers, pyramids and golden treasures.

The tourism industry is extremely important to the economy, bringing money and jobs. However, it has suffered in recent years. Terrorist attacks deterred visitors, as did the uprisings and the political uncertainties that followed the events of 2011.

DID YOU KNOW? Ancient Egyptians buried their pharaohs in a secret graveyard, known as the Valley of the Kings. The pharaohs were placed in hidden tombs, along with their treasures.

▼ The great rock temple of Rameses II at Abu Simbel, on Lake Nasser, is one of the most popular tourist attractions.

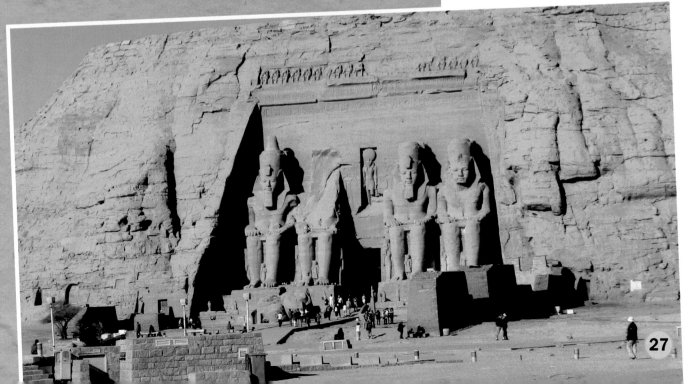

Environment and wildlife

Egypt is home to two wildlife extremes. The harsh desert environment is challenging to most living things. Coral reefs, however, support a huge range of animals.

Red Sea

Coral reefs around the Red Sea are teeming with wildlife. These structures are formed by tiny animals called polyps, and they create the perfect habitat for all sorts of animals, from small worms to large sharks. As elsewhere in the world, Egyptian reefs are under threat from environmental problems. Changes in water temperature and pollution kill the polyps and destroy reefs.

Egypt's coral reefs attract tourists who enjoy scuba diving and snorkelling at the Red Sea holiday resorts. If damage to the reefs continues, there may be a significant impact on tourism, as well as the natural environment.

Facts at a glance

Proportion of area protected: 5.7%

Biodiversity (known species): 2,700

Threatened species: 28

▼ Scuba diving around the coral reefs is an important part of the tourist industry, but divers must be very careful not to damage the fragile reef.

▶ Air pollution is contributing to the decay of many of Egypt's ancient limestone monuments, including the Sphinx.

Pollution

Pollution is an environmental issue that can have a devastating impact. The fumes from cars and gases produced during industrial processes and by burning waste contain tiny particles of dangerous substances. These toxins include soot, lead, carbon monoxide and sulphur dioxide.

These airborne pollutants contribute to human disease, especially lung diseases. Dirty water, often polluted with industrial and human waste, also damages health. Pollution kills wildlife too.

Turning to dust

When desertification occurs, fertile land loses its soil and turns into barren desert. It is a problem that affects many parts of North Africa, including Egypt. The United Nations predicts that Egypt will only be able to feed a quarter of its population by 2025 because of desertification.

It is also predicted that Egypt will have less freshwater in the future. More water may be extracted from the Nile before it even reaches Egypt, to irrigate farms in other countries. Also, global warming may result in an increase in sea level, which will cause seawater to move upstream, affecting irrigation and soil fertility around the Nile.

DID YOU KNOW?
Smog, or air pollution, sometimes reaches such high levels in Cairo that a black cloud of dirt descends on the city. It can hang over Cairo for weeks at a time.

Glossary

ancestors people you are descended from, before your grandparents

Byzantine Empire the eastern part of the Roman Empire after it split

circumcised when a boy has the foreskin of his penis removed as part of a religious ceremony

civil servants people who work for the government

delta where a river meets the sea and spreads out, forming lots of islands

desertification the loss of habitable land into desert

discrimination when people are treated badly because of their race or beliefs, for example

drought a shortage of rainfall

ethnic belonging to a particular human group with common traditions and culture

exports goods or services that are sold to another country

extended family members of a family beyond mother, father and their children

fertile land that is good for growing crops

flash flooding violent flooding that happens very quickly

freshwater inland water that is not salty

habitat the place where animals and plants live and exist

henna natural plant dye

hydroelectricity electricity produced by water power

illiterate unable to read or write

imports goods or services that are bought from another country

informal workers people who do not pay taxes to the government on the money they earn

irrigation a system of ditches and channels made to provide water to dry land

Moses in the Bible, the prophet who led the Hebrew people out of Egypt

nomadic people who move around rather than settling in one place

nuclear families families consisting of a mother, a father and their children

nutrients substances that all living things need to grow and survive

parasite something that depends on another living thing to survive, and is often harmful to it

persecution the poor treatment of one person or group by another

pharaohs kings or queens in ancient Egyptian times

raw materials resources such as timber and oil that are used to make products or other materials

rural to do with the countryside or agriculture

sanitation system that prevents the spread of disease by stopping humans coming into contact with waste material

slaughtered when an animal is killed for food

sultan the ruler of a Muslim country

technical skills skills needed to work in jobs such as engineering or computing

tectonic plates huge areas of rock beneath the Earth's crust that move very slowly, causing earthquakes and volcanoes when they rub against each other

terrorist someone who tries to put across their political or religious beliefs using violence

urban to do with towns and cities or life in towns and cities

utilities basic public services such as electricity, water supply and sewage disposal

vocational a job that someone is specially trained for

Topic web

Use this topic web to explore Egyptian themes
in different areas of your curriculum.

Design and Technology
The ancient Egyptians used a type of picture writing called hieroglyphics. Use the internet to look at some hieroglyphics and find out what they mean. Then design a hieroglyphic for your own name.

Maths
Find out how many Egyptian pounds there are in £1. How much would your favourite magazine cost in Egyptian pounds? What about a pint of milk and a loaf of bread?

History
Tutankhamun was less than 20 years old when he died, yet he is one of the most famous pharaohs of ancient Egypt. Find out more about King Tut. Why is he so well-known? What mystery surrounds his death? What treasures were found in his tomb?

Science
In ancient Egypt, the bodies of important people were preserved using a substance called natron. What is natron? Find out about the process of mummification. How did natron help preserve the bodies?

Egypt

Geography
The Nile is the longest river in the world. Find out where it begins and write down the names of the ten countries that it flows through.

English
Imagine you live in Egypt's capital, Cairo. Use the information in this book and any other resources available to write a short description of the city. What sights and sounds might you see and hear on your way to school?

Citizenship
In 2011, Egyptians protested about the way the government ran the country. Find out more about the protests. What rights and freedoms did the Egyptian people want?

ICT
Plan a visit to Egypt. Make a list of five places you would like to visit. Use the internet to work out how you can fly to Egypt and the best ways to get to each of your destinations.

Further information and index

Further reading

Egypt (World in Focus) by Jen Green (Wayland 2007)
Egypt in Our World by Ali Brownlie Bojang (Franklin Watts 2010)

Web

www.bbc.co.uk/news/world-africa-13313370
The BBC news page for Egypt, with recent events and background information.
https://www.cia.gov/library/publications/the-world-factbook/geos/eg.html
Information and statistics on Egypt, including geography, people and government.
/www.egypt.travel
The website of the Egyptian Tourist Authority, with information on places to visit, fairs and festivals.

Index